Rupert Murdoch

Rupert Murdoch is Chairman and Chief Executive Officer of News Corporation, one of the world's largest diversified media companies. News Corporation's global operations include newspaper and magazine publishing on three continents; significant book publishing interests; major motion picture and television production and distribution operations; and television, satellite and cable broadcast operations in the United States, Europe, Asia, Australia and Latin America.

In 1954, Mr. Murdoch took control of News Limited, an Australian-based public corporation whose only key asset at the time was a majority interest in the number-two daily newspaper in Adelaide, South Australia. Since then Mr Murdoch has overseen the expansion and development of the Company as it has become the most international of media businesses.

In 1960, the Company acquired the *Daily Mirror* in Sydney and, in 1964, launched a national newspaper, *The Australian*. In 1969, the Company ventured into the United Kingdom, acquiring the Sunday paper *News of the World* and later *The Sun* newspaper.

In the 1980s the Company purchased *The Times* and *Sunday Times* and HarperCollins Publishers, one of the world's largest and most prestigious book publishers. News Corporation's publishing interests now include capital city and suburban newspapers in Australia and the UK and *The New York Post* and *The Weekly Standard* in the US.

News Corporation purchased Twentieth Century Fox Film Corporation in 1985. The following year, the Company created the Fox Television Stations group—now comprising 35 stations across the United States—which formed the foundation for the launch of the Fox Broadcasting Company, now a leading U S television network. In October 1996, News Corporation launched the Fox News Channel, which is now the top-rating 24-hour news service in the United States. Also on American cable television, News Corporation has successfully established Fox Sports Net, FX and National Geographic Channel, Speed Channel, FUEL, and Fox Reality.

News Corporation is the major shareholder in British Sky Broadcasting, the UK's first satellite broadcasting operation, launched in 1989 and regarded as the world's most successful direct-to-home satellite broadcaster. And through its ownership of Hong Kong-based STAR, the first and only pan-Asian satellite broadcast service, acquired in 1993, News Corporation provides a variety of locally oriented programming services to more than 300 million people across Asia, the Indian sub-continent and the Middle East.

In 2005, News Corporation formed Fox Interactive Media to manage its growing stable of websites. The company then made a series of acquisitions including: MySpace.com, the world's largest social networking site; IGN Entertainment, a network of gaming and entertainment sites including RottenTomatoes.com; and Scout.com, the top collegiate and pro-sports online network.

Among News Corporation's other holdings are the inserts and consumer marketing group News America Marketing; 74 percent of conditional access company NDS; and, in 2007, News Corporation acquired Dow Jones & Company, including *The Wall Street Journal*.

Mr. Murdoch has been awarded the Companion of the Order of Australia (AC) for services to the media and to newspaper publishing in particular. Throughout News Corporation's history, he and his family have been closely involved with, and made generous contributions to, various educational, cultural, medical and charitable organizations throughout the United States, United Kingdom, Australia, Asia and Israel.

Mr. Murdoch is married and has six children.

Boyer Lectures

Each year the ABC invites a prominent Australian to present the result of his or her work and thinking on major social, scientific or cultural issues in a series of radio talks known as the Boyer Lectures. The series was inaugurated in 1959 under the title of ABC Lectures, but in 1961 was renamed as a memorial to the late Sir Richard Boyer who, as chairman of the ABC, had been one of those responsible for its introduction.

RUPERT
MURDOCH

A Golden Age of Freedom

The Boyer Lectures are broadcast each year on ABC Radio National's 'Big Ideas' program.

ABC Radio National is available throughout Australia on 260 transmitters including:

Adelaide 729AM
Brisbane 792AM
Canberra 846AM
Darwin 657AM
Gold Coast 90.1FM
Hobart 585AM
Melbourne 621AM
Newcastle 1512AM
Perth 810AM
Sydney 576AM

For your local frequency go to the ABC Radio National website at abc.net.au/rn or call 1300 13 9994 during working hours.

For ABC Radio National broadcast times and program details go to abc.net.au/rn or call listener enquiries on 02 8333 2821 during working hours.

RUPERT MURDOCH

A Golden Age of Freedom

Boyer Lectures 2007

ABC
Books

The cover image of 'The Stockman and His Family' by Russell Drysdale is reproduced by kind permission of The Drysdale Estate and News Corporation.

On page 27, four lines from Dorothea Mackellar's 'My Country' are reproduced by arrangement with the licencor, The Estate of Dorothea Mackellar, care of Curtis Brown (Aust.) Pty Ltd.

Published by ABC Books for the
AUSTRALIAN BROADCASTING CORPORATION
GPO Box 9994 Sydney NSW 2001

First published December 2008

ISBN 978 0 7333 2460 4.

Cover by Christabella Designs
Cover image courtesy of News Limited
Original cover design by Graham Rendoth/RENO Design Group
Text typeset in 11/18pt by Kirby Jones
Printed and bound in Australia by Griffin Press, Adelaide

5 4 3 2 1

contents

one
Aussie Rules: Bring back the pioneer

On the wall of my office at *The Wall Street Journal*, with its view across southern Manhattan to the Statue of Liberty in the haze-draped distance, I have an Australian painting that has travelled with me around the world. It is a work by Russell Drysdale. For me, it has a sentimental value beyond the artistic merit, but it also has flourishes of the theme I would like to discuss with you: Australia's place in this century of opportunity.

For those of you tragically unaware of the artistry of Drysdale, I suggest that you Google him. Drysdale was among the early modernists; in his day he became Australia's most famous artist. More than that, he was one of the first Australian artists to gain a truly international reputation. He did this with canvases that are at once utterly modern and distinctly Australian, with images that reflect the glory and the desolation of the outback.

Though he was slightly before my time, Drysdale and I attended the same boarding school outside Melbourne. We later became friends in Sydney. Born a decade after the Federation of Australia, he would live through two world wars, the postwar waves of European immigrants, the abolition of the White Australia Policy, and the growing emergence of a distinctly Australian nationalism. His paintings of soldiers, settlers, cane cutters and Indigenous people reflect this history.

The painting in my office is called *The Stockman and His Family*. It depicts a family using Drysdale's trademark red hues, and it captures the empathy of shared solitude. That solitude is a characteristic of our vast continent. I have vivid memories of long and dusty drives into the never-never. In its midst we are inevitably conscious of our individual smallness. Drysdale's sparseness inevitably prompts even the most thoughtless among us to contemplate this sense of unimportance.

When Drysdale's canvas catches my eye, it of course reminds me of home and of Australia's past and of my own past. It must be said that the protagonist is Aboriginal and his ancestors (our ancestors) experienced the vicissitudes and violence of nature long before the coming of European settlement. The continent was the same, the summers as unrelenting, the gums as ghostly. These are more than just shared circumstances but a common heritage, one that is denied in the dialectical deconstruction of the Aboriginal experience, for political points are too often scored at the expense of understanding.

But the scene with the stockman also points to the future. His family have clearly endured much hardship. They've been confronted by the heat and ochre dust in a way that few of us city slickers really experience, and yet there is a steeliness and closeness that suggest that this family is ready for the future. Our national character should never lose that steeliness.

We are all less innocent than we were 100 years ago. One of the most touching scenes in any small Australian town is the local war memorial, whether it is in the Mallee, out west, or up north. I suggest that every young Australian take a few moments to look at the names of those who left these towns and fought in distant wars. Can you possibly imagine what it was like for a lad to have left the wheat farm and found himself months later confronting a cliff and a machine gun in the Dardanelles? Today there is nothing sadder than visiting the graves of thousands of nineteen- and twenty-year-old Australians at Gallipoli.

My father, then a young war correspondent, was outraged by the mismatch between Australian enthusiasm and British logistical incompetence at Gallipoli. He was outraged, too, by the censorship that allowed that incompetence to continue to go unpunished. We were certainly less innocent after the Great War. But we must do more than just celebrate past heroism if we are to confront the future with confidence.

The First World War was the beginning of the end of our splendid isolation, and we have never been less isolated than we are now, ninety years later. Australia's identity is again undergoing dramatic change. We are fashioning it, and, in turn, it is being fashioned by external influences.

Our leading trade partners are the great nations of Asia, not mother England. European languages are generally less functional for our children than Chinese, Japanese and Indonesian, though I'd put in a special word for Spanish for its utility in Latin America and the United States.

My theme for these lectures is the great transformation we've seen in the past few decades, the unleashing of human talent and ability across our world, and the golden age for humankind that I see just around the corner. Over the course of the next five chapters, I will go into more detail about this golden age. I will talk about how the opening of new markets is leading to the rise of new nations and adding hundreds of millions of people to a new global middle class. I will address technology, education and the importance of cultivating human capital. I also hope to discuss what the information revolution means for the future of my own industry, especially newspapers. Most of all, I will speak of the challenges that all these developments pose for the land of my birth.

I appreciate that many Australians will argue whether I still have the right to call myself one of you. I was born in Melbourne, educated in Britain, and now make my home in Manhattan. My answer is that people can call me whatever they like, and, believe me when I tell you, they do. But this country means a great deal to me, and the main reason I agreed to come to Australia to deliver these lectures is that the country I see before me simply is not prepared for the challenges ahead.

As I write, in November 2008, the Australian economy is coming up against one of these challenges: a financial crisis whose origins are overseas. In recent weeks, the Australian dollar has fluctuated as wildly as a Whirling Dervish, and the impact is beginning to be felt in the real economy. There is no use bemoaning the problem. In this new century, Australia is wedded to the world—mostly for richer, very occasionally for poorer, certainly for better, and only rarely for worse. And I fear that many Australians will learn the hard way what it means to be unprepared for the challenges that a global economy can bring.

By most measures—the rule of law, economic performance and the quality of life—Australians today live in one of the most ideal societies on earth. Indeed, when *The Economist* listed the world's ten most livable cities, Australia had four of them: Melbourne, Perth, Adelaide and Sydney. That is a tremendous achievement, and an advantage in a world competing ferociously for talent and capital.

Here's my worry. While Australia generally does well in international rankings, those rankings can blind us to a larger truth. Australia will not succeed in the future if it aims to be just a bit better than average. Specifically, I believe that we need to revive the sense of Australia as a frontier country and to cultivate Australia as a great centre of excellence. Unlike our parents' and grandparents' times, this new frontier has little to do with the bush or the outback. Today the frontier we need to face is the wider world, and complacency is our chief enemy.

If you travel around Australia you will see that much of the country is in good shape. For example, while many farmers have had tough years of brown paddocks and harsh drought, the demand for our farm products will grow exponentially because of demand from around the globe.

Internationalisation means both opportunity and competition. It also means being clearer about the nature of Australia's identity, its qualities and its collective character. I'm not talking about re-embracing or re-creating the good old days of the past, I'm talking about what I hope will be the better days of the future.

A few months back I spent some time in both India and China. Between them, these two countries account for more than a third of the world's population. For most of my lifetime, the people of these great countries were incarcerated by communism or caste. In India's case, this was partly the result of long years of a kind of paternalistic socialism. Coupled with India's feudal system, its infamous bureaucracy, and its isolation from the global economy, there was a predictable outcome: Indian society had almost no upward mobility. If you were born poor, you were probably going to die poor.

China was even worse. After long misrule by centuries of autocrats, the arrival of communism supposedly promised liberation. Instead, the communists purged the entrepreneurs, industrialists and writers, and Mao's policies brought the nation to starvation, spiritual as well as physical. Then, in late 1978, Deng Xiaoping famously opened China's door to the world. Though China has a long way to go before it is a truly open society, the Chinese people have been using their new economic freedoms to accomplish extraordinary things.

In sheer numbers, the emergence of India and China as economic powers—and the wealth that they are creating—is accompanied by a rise of a new middle class. Over the next thirty years or so, two or three billion people will join this new global middle class. The world has never seen this kind of advance before. These are people who have known deprivation, these are people who are intent on developing their skills, improving their lives and showing the world what they can do. And they live right in Australia's neighbourhood.

The alarmists will tell you that Australia cannot compete with these nations. That is rubbish. In this new world, Australia has many advantages. These advantages include being an open, democratic and multiracial society, built on the rule of law. We have great resources as a civil society with a tradition of generosity and support. To compete well and use our human capital to the best, we will have to draw on these advantages and make our country stronger. That means being less dependent on government, less complacent about our national institutions, more willing to accept radical reform, and more trusting in our creativity and our competence.

I want to start by addressing some of these issues at home. By this I mean a need to reduce dependency on government, to reform our education system, to reconcile with Australia's Aboriginal population, and to maintain a liberal immigration system.

Let me start with dependency on government. At a time when the world's most competitive nations are moving their people off government subsidy, Australians seem to be headed in the wrong direction. In a recent paper, Des Moore, Director of the Institute of Private Enterprise and a former Deputy Secretary of Treasury, pointed out that while real incomes increased since the end of the 1980s, about 20 per cent of the working aged population today receives income support, compared to only 15 per cent two decades ago. While a safety net is warranted for those in genuine need, we must avoid institutionalising idleness. The bludger should not be our national icon.

Traditionally the Liberals have been more free market in their outlook than their opponents. But the Labor Party has also recognised that central planning does not work: the larger the government, the less room for Australians to exercise their talents and initiative. That is why earlier this year we heard a Labor Prime Minister, Kevin Rudd, declaring that his government is unashamedly pro-market, pro-business and pro-globalisation. That's a good start, but being pro-market, pro-business and pro-globalisation means working for a society where citizens are not dependent on the government. That means ending subsidies for people who do well.

It also means sensible targeting and persistence so that it will help those passing through a rough patch or born into abject poverty build themselves up to a point where they can provide for themselves. And it means smaller government and an end to the paternalism that nourishes political correctness, promotes government interference and undermines freedom and personal responsibility. Remember, it's not the Australian government that competes in the global market, it's Australian businesses and workers. With the relatively small domestic market, Australian workers and Australian businesses must be able to beat the best of the world.

Second, we need to reform our education system. In a later chapter I will go into more detail, but the bottom line is this: it is an absolute scandal that we are spending more and more on education and getting fewer and fewer results in return. For those still in school or just entering the workforce, the opportunities a global economy offers are greater than at any time in our history, provided you have the right skills.

Australians have always been a people who stress equality, who believe that what you make of yourself is more important than where you came from. That's still a good philosophy for a frontier society, but let's be honest: tens of thousands of Australians are going to be deprived of these opportunities if we continue to tolerate a public education system that effectively writes off whole segments of Australians.

In short, our country has a twenty-first century economy but only a nineteenth-century education system, and it is leaving too many children behind. That is an injustice to these citizens, and could make them a future burden on Australian society.

And school reform leads me to the next domestic priority: full reconciliation among all Australians. We are now beyond the day when Australian governments would take Aboriginal babies from their mothers' arms and hand them over to be raised by white Australians. Even that action was inspired as much by ignorance as arrogance. Many of the missionaries of the past were full of good intent but simply did not understand or respect Aboriginal culture.

Members of both major parties have each made eloquent and clear-headed statements expressing regret for the historic injustices visited on Aboriginal Australians. That there were victims, and many of them, is beyond dispute. But apologies alone will not achieve true reconciliation, and neither will allowing victimhood to remain dominant in our national psyche. Far from liberating our Aboriginal brothers and sisters from the colonial yoke, we have cultivated a well-intentioned but stultifying dependency.

The best way to redress the past and advance true equality is to ensure that the next generation of Aboriginal children has access to top quality schools and teachers, which they do not now have. Australia's system of public education can never be called a success until Aboriginal Australians benefit from it as much as any other citizens.

At the same time, however, we cannot avert our eyes to the abuse of women and children within Aboriginal communities. These are not simple problems, but they will remain serious ones until our response is informed more by true compassion and less by remorse.

Finally, Australia will be strong only if it is open to others, to immigration. Thank goodness we are beyond where we were a few decades ago. Even though we opened our borders to southern Europe and other non-Anglo populations after the Second World War, it was not until after the Vietnam War that we began welcoming our neighbours in the region. Now, in a relatively short period of time we have buried 'White Australia' and raised a modern, diverse society in its place.

This does not mean we are neutral or valueless. We must expect immigrants to learn our language and embrace the principles that make Australia a decent and tolerant nation.

At the same time, Australia needs to recognise that immigrants bring energy, skills and enthusiasm. They often better recognise the virtues of Australian society, virtues that we are too shy or embarrassed to laud.

In my view, Australians should not worry when other people want to come to our country. The day to worry is when immigrants are *no longer* attracted to our shores. We should be a beacon to all. To our region in particular, we should be a living, happy, civil and contesting democracy that is a model for the emerging democracies around us.

These are priorities for Australia on the home front. But in foreign affairs Australia also has a role to play. Part of this role is to ensure that Australian interests are represented and advanced internationally. In the twenty-first century we must lead rather than react. In trade, for example, Australia is one of the few resource-rich societies that has embraced the open market. In many ways, our experience is the exception rather than the rule. Generally when nations have resources they sit back and savour these resources rather than do the hard work of building a competitive economy around them.

Today Australia probably leads the world in freedom in that area of trade most restricted around the world— agriculture. Restrictions on agriculture hurt many of the world's poorest nations, and we have both a moral and strategic interest in seeing them lifted. So we must continue to leverage our trading relationships and continue to push when others have left the conference table. The global trade dialogue should echo with Australian accents.

Climate change is another area where Australia needs to lead rather than follow. I'm not sold on the more apocalyptic visions of climate change, but I do believe that the planet deserves the benefit of the doubt. I believe there will be great rewards for those Australians who discover new ways of reducing emissions or cleaning the environment. Here at News in Australia we are encouraging that process through an initiative called 'One Degree'. It's about every one of our people making small changes that together make a big difference. This program is part of a larger corporate initiative that is designed with a clear goal, to have all of our businesses around the world carbon neutral by 2010, and we are counting on the talents and creativity of all our employees to meet that goal.

The emphasis should be on practical solutions. We cannot address climate change merely with emotion. The ultimate solution is not to punish the Australian economy by imposing standards that the rest of the world will never meet, but to take the lead in developing real alternatives by offering clean, cheap energy to meet the growing demand. The world desperately needs these cleaner and more abundant sources of energy. That will require huge investments in new technology. But the upside is huge. If we can develop cleaner and cheaper sources of energy we will grow our economy while leaving a greener, cleaner world for our children and grandchildren.

Our world remains a dangerous place. In this promising new century we are still seeing naked, heartless aggression, whether it comes from a terrorist bombing in Islamabad or a Russian invasion of Georgia. At the same time, our traditional allies in Europe sometimes seem to have lost the will to confront aggression, even on their own doorstep. We can lament these developments, but we cannot hide from them. The fact is that throughout our past, Australian lives have always been affected by events in distant and unfamiliar places. That will remain true for the future as well. We need to be prepared to respond to these threats, as we have done in Iraq and are doing in Afghanistan.

But we need to be more than a reliable partner that the United States can call on. Australia needs to be part of a reform of the institutions most responsible for maintaining peace and stability. I'm thinking especially of NATO.

Although NATO was designed to prevent a land war in Europe, it is now fighting well beyond its borders. As can be seen in Afghanistan, not everyone is doing their share, and that is a problem too many people want to ignore.

The only path to reform NATO is to expand it to include nations like Australia. That way NATO will become a community based less on geography and more on common values. That is the only way NATO will be effective, and Australian leadership is critical to these efforts.

Finally, there is an even more fundamental constitutional question about our identity. Should Australia be a republic? There has been more maturity to this debate over the past couple of years, and there is now no need to rush to the exit. But the moment is not far away when the country will decide its fate, and if I were in a position to vote, it would be for a republic. The establishment of a republic of Australia will not slight the Queen, nor will it deny the British traditions, values and structures that have served us so well. But we are no longer a dependency and we should be independent.

In this young century we should assert our personality. We alone must define our future. An independent Australia will have no excuses for failure because the mistakes will be all our own. But I have few doubts that we will prosper because I have much confidence in this country and its people.

Hidden away in Dorothea Mackellar's best known poem, *My Country*, is a description of the land of my birth that means much to me:

> *An opal-hearted country,*
> *A wilful, lavish land—*
> *All you who have not loved her,*
> *You will not understand—*

two
Who's Afraid of New Technology?

The word 'technology' has a coldness and a distance that seems removed from human experience. Indeed, the term 'high technology' sounds almost religious, while the 'techies' are like the high priests who are sometimes almost a little *too* expert in the art of technology.

Fears about technology and the change it brings are nothing new. But today these changes are accelerating, and their impact is a mix of the miraculous, the efficacious and the disorienting. Sentimentality sometimes blocks our path to the future. And it's always tempting to romanticise the rustic.

So I have a simple and provocative proposition: whingeing about technology will get you nowhere. The only way to deal with new technology which up-ends your job or your business model is to get out in front of it because otherwise it will get out in front of you.

Now, I'm not saying that we should all become card-carrying geeks. But we do need to be contemporary—and to comprehend the impact on our family and our society.

A little later, I will explain why I believe that technology—for all the disruptions it is causing—is, on balance, a very good thing. But before I do, I'd like to begin with a story about some of Australia's convicts. You may not know this, but many of these were people who came to our country because of the technological changes of their day. I hope their story will provide a little historical perspective on the disruptions we're all feeling in our own age.

The people I have in mind lived in the late eighteenth and very early nineteenth centuries. They were from the western part of England, and they worked in textiles. In other words, they were typical English countrymen living just before the Industrial Revolution. They worked mostly out of their own homes, alongside their families, and the prices and practices for their trade were set by long-standing regulation.

Then something happened that shook this tidy little world to its core. In the late 1700s, a series of labour-saving inventions turned the status quo on its head. These early machines were crude, and in terms of quality, they were no match for the best cloths produced by skilled artisans.

But they had a crucial advantage: they could produce cloth that was cheap. That was because they did not require as much manpower. Another way of putting this is that the new technology allowed textile producers to be more productive. And consumers benefited because they had access to lower priced clothing and textiles.

However, the traditional textile workers saw the new technology as a threat. So in 1811 they organised themselves and threatened to destroy the mills and machinery of the owners who used it to produce lower-priced goods.

The threats were issued under the name of 'General Ludd' or 'King Ludd'. Ludd was apparently a local folk hero who had destroyed two stocking frames in an earlier (1779) attack in Leicestershire. And the 'luddites', as they called themselves, didn't just threaten. They backed up their threats with physical attacks. So fierce were the attacks that the British government made the destruction of machinery a capital crime, and in 1812 sent thousands of British troops to put down the workers' rebellion.

In many ways the workers' distress was understandable. The new technology turned their world upside down. It took them out of their homes, where they operated as independent contractors, and into the factory, where they were paid wages. It moved them from the countryside to the city. In the end, this new technology would help make the British textile industry a world leader. But the disruptions were real and painful.

A number of the leading luddites were arrested and brought to a mass trial. Some were hanged. Some were thrown into prison. And some were transported here to Australia, where they were among our first settlers. They were treated very harshly. But they were truly prisoners of the past.

Today, attitudes are a little different. Except for the occasional mad Frenchman who leads an assault on a local McDonald's, nowadays luddites do not go in for physical attacks. Yet in many countries, people are facing similar disruptions driven by technology—to their business models, to their livelihoods, to their homes and communities. We are in an era of unprecedented creative destruction, but there is far more being created than there is being destroyed.

My own industry—news and entertainment—is certainly feeling the impact. As we are in the midst of a shift from an industrial society to an information society, the news and entertainment industry is right in the centre of the maelstrom. For me, personally, it has been a learning experience. And for us, collectively, the journey is just beginning.

Think about the Wall Street trader—at least, the one who still has a job—who now has instantaneous access to 'real time' prices around the world. Then there is the South Korean teenager who uses MySpace to download music and chat with a German friend who shares her taste in bands. Or the research scientist in Bangalore in India who can tap into the expertise of the best minds from around the world to help on a project to improve crop yields in the poorest parts of India.

Yet even the beneficiaries worry that technology is more controlling than controlled. Workers fret for their jobs, not only fearing that they might lose them, but they that they will be superseded by a younger generation. Governments worry about people having access to information they no longer control. Corporate executives, who once enjoyed quasi-monopolies, now lose sleep, fearing that some little icon on someone's desktop is going to wipe out their entire business.

And then there are the couples whose marriages are in turmoil because the executive sleeps with a buzzing Blackberry by the bedside and compulsively answers email at the breakfast table.

As chief executive of a global media and entertainment company, I can tell you that I feel these challenges daily. Technology is destroying the business models we have relied on for decades. This is especially true for those whose business models have been based on a one-size-fits-all approach to their customers.

Think, for example, of the giant American television networks that are finding their mass audience shrinking with every passing day. Why? Because people suddenly have a growing multitude of choices—and they are rightly exercising those choices.

Let me give you another example, one that is painful for those who own and love newspapers. In the old days, a crucial source of revenue for a local newspaper was its classified advertisements. If you wanted to sell your car or rent out an apartment, the classifieds were about your only choice of matching a buyer or seller.

But in little more than a decade, this model has become obsolete. The near-monopoly that newspaper classifieds once enjoyed has been overtaken by websites like craigslist and realestate.com. For consumers, this is good news because it's become easier and cheaper for you to buy or sell what you want. But it is costing newspapers millions in vital revenues that they used to take for granted.

In this environment, it's understandable that people on the losing end worry about where the information revolution is taking us. So it can be easy to become pessimistic about the future.

But I believe technology is ushering in a new golden age for humankind. I also believe that technology is making the human side of the business equation—skills and knowledge— more valuable than ever. And I believe that societies that want to prosper in this new age need to cultivate a spirit of learning and flexibility and achievement.

So I would like to consider three subjects. First, why technology is a good thing despite the unsettling changes it brings. Second, in business terms, how technology is putting a greater premium on what is awkwardly called 'human capital'. Finally, I want to say something about what this means for Australia's future.

Let me start with why advances in information technology are a good thing. As these advances challenge the accepted ways of doing things, businesses are going to have to work harder to keep their customers. That includes companies like mine, and consumers like you.

The challenge is clear. But so is history. Each improvement in information technology we have seen in the past—beginning with Gutenberg's press and continuing with radio and television—has opened up access to more news and entertainment for millions of people who previously couldn't receive or afford it. There is no reason to think the trend will be different this time. Except that this time, the access will be universal and the impact will be more profound.

History also shows that with each new advance, existing businesses are forced to become more creative and relevant to their customers. Once upon a time, the media and entertainment companies could count on the necessary, huge, up-front investments to discourage competitors from entering the business. But now, in many sectors, the cost barriers to entry have never been lower—and the opportunities for the energetic and the creative have never been greater.

Competition is becoming more intense every day because technology now allows the little guy to do what once required a huge corporation. Look at the Drudge Report.

Matt Drudge doesn't really create content. Instead, he finds material that he thinks is interesting, and puts it up on one of the internet's simplest pages. Readers come because they trust his judgment. And he is showing that good news judgment is something that can add value.

Even those who don't like him—including many editors and reporters—click on to his website every day. In other words, with his single web page, Drudge has succeeded in challenging all the leading media companies of our day—including mine. And he has done it all with minimal start-up costs: a computer, a modem and some space on a server.

When someone uses technology this way, consumers benefit. And it's not just the internet that allows this to happen. Just think of all the things that you can do now because of technology—things that would have been impossible just twenty years ago.

If you want to find out the status of a trade bill in the United States Congress, you can access it from your desktop. If you are a footy fan living in Jakarta, you can click on to the *Melbourne Herald Sun* and see how the Cats did against the Hawks. If you are in Dubai and you want to know the euro–dollar rate and make a trade a few seconds later, it's never been easier to make or to lose money.

In other words, you can do more of what you want to do—and you can do it in less time and at less cost. That makes you more efficient. When you apply these marginal improvements across an entire country, profits are increased, friends are made, and the traditionally disadvantaged have greater access to information than at any time in our shared history.

The market encourages the spread of technology because businesses have an incentive to attract more and more customers. That's why technological breakthroughs that start out as expensive luxuries quickly become everyday necessities. In 2008, for example, in India and China alone 200 million mobile phones will be sold.

But technology will do you no good unless you have men and women who know how to take advantage of it. Which leads me to my second point: the growing importance of human capital; in other words, the need for an educated and adaptable population.

As technology levels the playing field, the human factor becomes more important. In plain English, if you run a business, you need good people more than ever.

That's because computers will never substitute for common sense and good judgment. They will never have empathy either. To be successful, a business needs people who see the big picture, who can think critically, and who have strong character.

Economists call these skills 'human capital'. You won't find this capital listed on a corporate balance sheet. But it is the most valuable asset a company has. If you talk to any chief executive about his number one challenge today, he will probably not say technology. It's far more likely he will say his top challenge is attracting and retaining talented people.

Back in 1992, Bill Gates talked about this in an interview with *Forbes* magazine. Here's how he put it: 'Take our twenty best people away, and I tell you that Microsoft would become an unimportant company.'

In other words, what separates Microsoft from the competition isn't software—it's human beings. That is why companies these days invest so heavily in helping employees develop their talents and sharpen their skills. Just as you need to refurbish plants and take care of other assets, if you want to keep your company in the lead, you need to invest in your people.

If you are a worker, you have an even greater incentive to invest in yourself. We are long past the day when you took a job at a company and then forty years later retired after doing more or less the same thing every day, day after day. That kind of mediocrity has been banished.

My point is this: as technology advances, the premium for educated people with talent and judgment will increase. In the future, successful workers will be those who embrace a lifetime of learning. Those who don't will be left behind.

That may sound harsh. But it is a truth we must face. And it is a great opportunity for us all.

For most people, adapting to the changes that are coming will require moving out of comfort zones. And moving out of comfort zones begins with education.

I will say more about education in a later chapter, but I want to emphasise here that if we want to build an Australia where people are *not* left behind, we need to recognise that a first-class education is no longer a luxury. In our age, it is a fundamental civil right and necessity. The most important skill our children will need in their careers is the ability to acquire new skills. At an absolute minimum, that means that every Australian ought to leave secondary school with a basic mastery of reading, writing and arithmetic. They should also have a love of learning and a sense of their own potential. And for that cherished outcome we need teachers who inspire—not those who conspire to thwart change.

But secondary education is only the bare minimum. At all levels, we need to set high standards—and stick to them. At least in science, Australia has a pretty strong tradition. Of the ten Nobel prizes that have been awarded to Australians since 1915, nine were for science or medicine. Two other Australian scientists have won Nobel prizes for work they did overseas. Another two Nobel winners have strong connections with Australia.

This list of Nobel laureates includes the father and son team of William and Laurence Bragg (Physics, 1915), Howard Walter Florey (Medicine, 1945), Frank McFarlane Burnet (Medicine, 1960), and Barry Marshall and Robin Warren (both for Medicine, 2005). I am not a scientist, so I won't pretend to understand the research for which they won their prizes, but I do know that their contributions have helped turn penicillin into a lifesaver, revolutionised treatment for gastro-duodenal ulcers, and provided the foundation for modern biotechnology and genetic engineering.

In Australia today we have many fine scientific research centres, but we have no large international centres of excellence. As a small nation, we will never be competitive in every sphere. But there is no excuse for failing to cultivate areas where we enjoy an advantage and where talented people from around the world are fighting to get in. And we need to buttress this advantage with the legal, business and social environments designed to support a culture of excellence.

In the past few years, Australian governments have made some strides in this direction, even though Australia is a small country without the cushion of a large domestic market. Yet we need to do more than catch up. We need to lead—by example and by results.

This is where our sense of comfort can be a formidable enemy. Sometimes the most established countries are the most vulnerable—because people in other parts of the world have more incentive to innovate. For example, mobile phone technology has proliferated rapidly in countries such as India, China and Africa because people were fed up with the long wait they had for a land line. The result has been that some of the less developed nations have leapfrogged over us in areas such as per capita reach of high-speed broadband.

For much of the past few decades, a good part of Australia's domestic debate has focused on immigration. Australia has done a reasonably good job of absorbing those who share our values and aspirations. At the same time, I believe we don't worry nearly enough about the flip side: whether Australia will build the kind of society that can and will continue to attract talented people from the outside—not to mention keeping the ones we have.

This capability will grow even more important in the future, and the reason has to do with a fact of human nature: when people are linked to the outside world, they begin to make comparisons. They travel and see what the opportunities are like elsewhere. And they begin thinking about where they want to live and work and raise their families.

Right now Australia has many advantages—a democratic government, a relatively open economy, a beautiful environment, and a fundamentally tolerant society. In contrast, many of the world's most talented and ambitious are coming from societies that are unfree, where their cities are clogged with pollution, and where they enjoy few of the amenities we take for granted in Australia. But trade and technology means these countries are catching up with us—and they are catching up fast.

None of this is to deny that technology can't be abused. The same technology that puts mobile phones within reach of people with less money by making them disposable can also be used by criminals to evade the police. The same internet that allows you to order the latest bestseller online also allows sex predators to trawl for victims in relative anonymity. And the same payment systems that allow you to buy something electronically help international drug lords to launder money.

These are all challenges that must be addressed. But just as we don't ban automobiles because thieves use cars to flee a crime scene, and we don't ban telephones because some people use them to make obscene calls, we are not going to give up the advantages other technologies offer just because some people abuse them.

I am one of those who believe that free societies are more than capable of addressing the problems created by technology. And I have great faith that Australia can harness its potential to expand opportunity, promote freedom and bring a better quality of life. Our motto has always been 'she'll be right'—but she'll be right only if we *make* it right.

three
The Future of Newspapers: Moving beyond dead trees

There is a subject that always gets certain journalists going: the future of newspapers. It's a subject that has relevance far beyond the feverish, sometimes insecure collection of egos and energy that is the journalistic profession.

Too many journalists seem to take a perverse pleasure in ruminating on their pending demise. Although a number of industries today are facing stiff new competition from the internet—banks, retailers, phone companies, and so on— these sectors also regard the internet as an extraordinary opportunity. But among our journalistic friends are some misguided cynics who are too busy writing their own obituaries to be excited by that opportunity.

Self-pity is never pretty. Sometimes it even starts in journalism school, some of which are perpetuating the pessimism of their tribal elders. But I have a very different view: unlike the doom and gloomers, I believe that newspapers will reach new heights. In the twenty-first century, people are hungrier for information than ever before. And they have more sources of information than ever before.

Amid these many diverse and competing voices, readers want what they've always wanted: a source they can trust. That has always been the role of great newspapers in the past. And that role will make newspapers great in the future.

If you discuss the future with newspapermen, you will find that too many think that our business is only in physical newspapers. I like the look and feel of newsprint as much as anyone, but our real business isn't printing on dead trees; it's showing great judgment and giving our readers great journalism.

It's true that in the coming decades, the printed versions of some newspapers will lose circulation. But if papers provide readers with news they can trust, we'll see gains in circulation—on our web pages, through our RSS feeds, in emails delivering customised news and advertising to mobile phones.

The Future of Newspapers: Moving beyond dead trees

In short, we are moving from news *papers* to news *brands*. For all of my working life, I have believed that there is a social and commercial value in delivering accurate news and information in a cheap and timely way. As this century develops, the form of delivery may change, but the potential audience for our content will multiply many times over.

The news business is very personal for me. For more than a half century, newspapers have been at the heart of my business. If I am sceptical about the pessimists today, it's because of a simple reason: I have heard their morose soothsaying many times before.

The challenges are real. There will probably never be a paperless office, but young people are starting to live in paperless homes. Traditional sources of revenue—such as classifieds—are drying up, putting pressure on the business model. And journalists face new competition from alternative sources of news and information.

Therefore we have a steady stream of stories coming from reputable sources like *The Economist*, with covers declaring that 'newspapers are now an endangered species'. That's quite ironic coming from a successful and growing magazine that likes to describe itself as 'a newspaper'.

My summary of the way some of the established media has responded to the internet is this: it's not newspapers that might become obsolete; it's some of the editors, reporters and proprietors who are forgetting a newspaper's most precious asset—the bond with its readers.

When I was growing up, this was the key lesson my father impressed on me. The best thing an owner could do was to hire editors who looked out for the readers' interests, and to give these readers good honest reporting on issues that mattered most to them. In return, you would be rewarded with trust and loyalty you could take to the bank.

Over many decades in newspapers I have been privileged to witness history being made and printed almost every night. There is a lot these experiences have taught me—and it gives me confidence about the future.

I would like to use my experience to illuminate the way we need to respond to the two most serious challenges facing newspapers today. One of these is the competition that is coming from new technology—especially the internet. But the more serious challenge is the complacency and condescension that festers at the heart of some newsrooms. The complacency stems from having enjoyed a monopoly, and now finding they have to compete for an audience they once took for granted.

The Future of Newspapers: Moving beyond dead trees

The condescension that many show their readers is an even bigger problem. It takes no special genius to point out that if you are contemptuous of your customers, you are going to have a hard time getting them to buy your product. Newspapers are no exception.

I became an editor and owner well before I had planned. It happened when my father died, and I was called home from Oxford. That was how I found myself a newspaper proprietor at the age of twenty-two. I was so young and so new to the business that when I pulled my car into the car park on my first day, the garage attendant admonished me, 'Hey, sonny, you can't park here'.

That paper was *The News* in Adelaide. Its newsroom was a noisy place. But it was noise with purpose. The chattering and pounding of typewriter keys reached a crescendo in the minutes before a deadline that was stretched beyond breaking point by gun reporters determined to get the latest, freshest version of a story.

That background music created an urgency all of its own. When the presses began to run, everyone in the building felt the rumble. And when the presses were late, the journalists felt *me* rumble.

When I took over *The News*, *The Adelaide Advertiser* was the dominant paper in town. Its owners tried to get my mother to sell to them. They sent her a letter basically saying that if she didn't accept their offer, they were going to put *The News* out of business. We responded by printing their letter on the front page of our paper.

The result of that action was a good old-fashioned stoush—a newspaper war. It cost a great deal. But it taught me that with good editors and a loyal readership, you can challenge better-heeled and more established rivals—and succeed. And we did.

A decade later, there was another test: creating Australia's first national paper. That might not sound like a big deal today. But back in the 1960s it was, when the country was only barely linked by phone lines. Our plan was to start a paper in Canberra, build it—and then take it national.

If the technological challenges were not daunting enough, our competitors got wind of our plans. As soon as they did, they transformed the existing paper—*The Canberra Times*—into a pretty impressive broadsheet. By doing that, they hoped to grab readers and advertisers before we could even get off the ground. There was only one way to respond: we had to go national almost two years ahead of schedule.

Today, of course, even the smallest Australian newspaper has a web page that you can log in to from Cairns to Caracas. But back then, we didn't even have reliable fax lines. Instead, we had to fly the printing plates from Canberra to presses elsewhere in the country—usually late at night. We even started up our own air service to do it.

It was all pretty complex and, of course, things did not always go to plan. But it was also exhilarating. The result was that we brought readers across Australia a better, more informative product, and helped transform Australian journalism.

It was also excellent preparation for the next big fight we had: the opening of our new presses at Wapping in England.

For those who are too young to remember those daunting days, let me give you some perspective. Back in the mid-1980s, British papers were essentially run by their unions, and these unions resisted all improvements.

These were not unions acting on behalf of the working class, but a cosy, corrupt closed shop. Some of the names that drew pay cheques didn't even exist. Our payroll showed that cheques were being sent to people like M. Mouse and D. Duck—neither of whom paid income tax.

At a time when new printing technology was making other papers around the world more efficient, newspapers in Britain were forced to rely on a technology that had not changed much since Gutenberg's Bible. The costs were forcing the loss of hundreds of jobs and crippling what is now the world's most vibrant newspaper market.

In the long run it was not sustainable. *The Times'* columnist Bernard Levin described Fleet Street this way: 'Conditions which combined a protection racket with a lunatic asylum.'

So we decided to change it. We bought new, state-of-the-art presses, installed them at a site away from Fleet Street, in Wapping, to the east of the City, and found good people to run them.

In the end, it was expensive. There was terrible violence, especially against the police. Those workers who chose to fight the move and the changes expected that management would roll over as so many managements had in the past. And for a few weeks, we were literally under siege by people intent on damaging our presses, hurting our people and killing our business.

The Future of Newspapers: Moving beyond dead trees

But we had planned well, and we prevailed. Our victory helped make all British newspapers more profitable. And of course this meant better wages and a brighter future for their employees.

Today the challenge we face is different. In some ways, it is a direct attack on our editorial judgment.

It used to be that a handful of editors could decide what was news—and what was not. These men acted rather like demigods. If they ran a story, it became news. If they ignored an event, it never happened.

Today, though, editors are losing this power. The internet, for example, provides access to thousands of news sources that cover things an editor might ignore. And if you aren't satisfied with that, you can start up your own blog and cover and comment on the news yourself.

Traditional journalists like to think of themselves as watchdogs, but they haven't always responded well when the public calls them to account.

When veteran news anchor and contributor to US '60 Minutes' Dan Rather broadcast his story suggesting President Bush had evaded service during his days in the National Guard, bloggers quickly exposed the dubious nature of his sources and documents.

Yet far from celebrating this citizen journalism, the establishment media reacted defensively. During an appearance on Fox News, a CBS executive attacked the bloggers in a statement that will go down in the annals of arrogance.

'60 Minutes', he said, was a professional organisation with 'multiple layers of checks and balances'. By contrast, he dismissed the blogger as 'a guy sitting in his living room in his pyjamas, writing'. But eventually it was the guys sitting in their pyjamas who forced Mr Rather and his producer to resign.

Dan Rather and his defenders are not alone. A recent American study reported that many editors and reporters simply do not trust their readers to make good decisions. Let's be clear about what this means: it is a polite way of saying that these editors and reporters think their readers are too stupid to think for themselves.

By taking their audience for granted and allowing themselves to become as institutionalised as any government or company they write about, these journalists are threatening their own papers. It is simply extraordinary that so many who are privileged to sit in the front row and write the first account of history could be so immune to its obvious meaning—not to mention the consequences for their own industry.

Let me give you an example. Four years ago the circulation of *The Times* of London was falling somewhat. So we experimented with changing from a broadsheet to what we call a 'compact' version. For almost a year, we printed two versions of *The Times*—each with the same photos, the same headlines and the same stories.

By an overwhelming margin, readers preferred the compact version. So we adopted that version, reversed our decline in circulation, and helped put *The Times* on a more solid footing, which, of course, is the key to keeping jobs. And we did it without affecting the quality of the news.

You might think our experience with *The Times* would be a good lesson about responding to what readers want, and keeping a newspaper relevant and viable. But that's not what most journalists wrote about. Instead, they offered a lot of hand-wringing about 'tradition'—and sentimental laments for a format that most *Times*' readers no longer cared for.

I see the same thing every day. Instead of finding stories that are relevant to their readers' lives, papers run stories reflecting the interests of their editors and journalists. Instead of writing for their audience, they are writing for their colleagues. And instead of commissioning stories that will gain them readers, some editors commission stories the sole purpose of which is the quest for a prize.

When I started out in the business, anyone who dared parade a prize for excellence would have been hooted out of the newsroom for taking himself too seriously. But today the desire for awards has become a fetish. Papers may be losing money, losing circulation and laying off people left and right, but they will have a wall full of awards—prisoners of the past rather than enthusiasts for the future.

Readers want news as much as they ever did. Today *The Times* of London is read by a diverse global audience of 26 million people each month. That is an audience larger than the entire population of Australia—an audience whose sheer size is beyond the comprehension and ambitions of its founders in 1785. That single statistic tells you that there is a discerning audience for news.

The operative word is discerning. To compete in journalism today, you can't offer the old one-size-fits-all approach.

These days, the defining digital trend in content is the increasing sophistication of search. You can already customise your news flow, whether by country, company or subject. A decade from now, the offerings will be even more sophisticated. You will be able to satisfy your unique interests and search for unique content.

After all, a female university student in Malaysia is not going to have the same interests as a sixty-year-old Manhattan executive. Closer to home, your teenage son is not going to have the same interests as your mother. The challenge is to use a newspaper's brand while allowing readers to personalise the news for themselves—and then deliver it in the ways that they want.

This is what we are now trying to do at *The Wall Street Journal*. The *Journal* has the advantage of having a very loyal readership, a brand known for quality, and editors who take the readers and their interest seriously.

This helps explain why the *Journal* continues to defy industry trends. Of the ten largest papers in the United States, the *Journal* is the only one to have increased its paid subscriptions last year.

Now we intend to make our mark on the digital frontier. The *Journal* is already the only US newspaper that makes real money online. One reason for this is a growing global demand for business news—and *accurate* business news. Integrity is not just a characteristic of the *Journal*, it is a selling point.

One way we are planning to take advantage of online opportunities is by offering three tiers of content. The first will be the news that we put online for free. The second will be available for those who subscribe to *wsj.com*. And the third will be a premium service, designed to give its customers the power to customise high-end financial news and analysis from around the world.

In all we do, we're going to deliver the news in ways that best fit our readers' preferences: on web pages they can access from home or work, on still evolving inventions like Amazon's kindle, as well as on mobile phones or Blackberries.

In the end, we are where we began: with the bond of trust between readers and their paper. Much has changed since I walked into *The News* in Adelaide in 1954. Presses have never been faster or more flexible. We have computers that allow you to lay out multiple pages in multiple countries. We have faster distribution. But none of it will mean anything for newspapers unless we meet our first responsibility: earning the trust and loyalty of our readers.

I do not claim to have all the answers. Given the realities of modern technology, the broadcast version of this chapter can be sliced and digitally diced. It can be accessed in a day or a month or a decade. And I can rightly be held to account in perpetuity for the points on which I am proven wrong—as well as mocked for my inability to see just how much more different the world had become.

But I don't think I will be proven wrong on one point. The newspaper, or a very close electronic cousin, will always be around. It may not be thrown on your front doorstep the way it is today. But the thud it makes as it lands will continue to echo around society and the world.

four
Fortune Favours the Smart

As a child, I attended boarding school outside Melbourne. Bucolic and idyllic, it wasn't. So I made myself a promise. I swore that I would never become one of those fogeys who goes on and on about how his schooldays were the best days of his life.

I intend to keep that promise, but I do want to talk about schools. In particular, I would like to talk about why you hear so many business leaders talking about the problems with public education. Far from reminiscing about some glorious and largely mythical past, I want to focus on the challenges we face today—and what they mean for our future.

Let me say at the outset: it is not a pretty picture.

The unvarnished truth is that in countries such as Australia, Britain, and particularly the United States, our public education systems are a disgrace. Despite spending more and more money, our children seem to be learning less and less—especially those who are most vulnerable in our society.

In my view, things will not really improve until we begin setting much higher expectations—for our students, for our teachers, and for our schools. At the very least, we ought to demand as much quality and performance from those who run our schools as we do from those who provide us with our morning cup of coffee. And then we ought to hold these schools accountable when they fail.

In Australia, we pride ourselves on our passion for equality; we have popularised the word 'egalitarian'. That passion is an attractive part of the Australian character. But it is getting harder and harder to square Australian pride in equality with the realities of the Australian system of public education.

Like me, many of you probably went to a decent school. Your children will probably do the same. This means that your family will probably thrive no matter what happens, because, no doubt, you have primed them to succeed. But too many children are socialised to fail.

We can argue over whether our better schools are as focused as they should be on mathematics and science. But it is inarguable that our lesser schools are leaving far too many children innumerate, illiterate and ignorant of our history. These are the people whose future I am most concerned about. For these boys and girls to rise in society—and have a fair go at the opportunities you and I take for granted—a basic education is essential.

The tragedy today is that in many nations like Australia, the people who need a solid education to lift them out of deprived circumstances are the people who are falling further and further behind. That is unacceptable to me. And it should be unacceptable to all of us.

So I will talk about three things. First, how the dividing line between the haves and the have-nots is no longer how much money they have. Increasingly, your life chances and your life choices will be defined by your skills and knowledge.

Second, why we need to stop making excuses for schools and school systems that are failing the very children they are meant to serve.

And finally, the need for corporations to become more involved—especially at the lower school levels. Corporate leaders know better than government officials the skills that people need to get ahead in the twenty-first century. And businessmen and businesswomen need to take this knowledge and help build school systems that will ensure that all children get at least a basic education.

Let me begin with the growing importance of education in our new economy. At first glance, it might look as though advances in technology are making education less important. After all, thanks to computers and calculators, even people without a good education now have the ability to have their sums done for them by a cheap calculator, to have their faulty spelling corrected by a word processing program, and to have even complex tasks completed for them by a specialised software program.

For example, if you go to a McDonald's or a corner shop the person behind the counter no longer has to calculate the change. The cash register is now a mini-computer and the barcode does the work.

In industry, computers and automation have reduced much of the need for calculation and repetitive labour. And, as unions in Europe have been quick to notice, that means many enterprises can be more productive with fewer workers. This in turn is one big reason that many unions—like the luddites before them—are so opposed to new technology.

But ultimately, fighting a new and better technology is a fool's errand. History clearly demonstrates that a technology that shows itself to be more productive will win out in the end. The reason is simple. Over the long haul, no one is going to pay more than he has to for something that can be done far more cheaply. Even if an individual businessman or two were willing to forego such an improvement, in the end they will be forced to adopt the more productive approach just to keep up with their competitors.

That's where a good education comes in. New technology is replacing many tedious tasks. That means there will be fewer and fewer satisfying jobs for people without skills. In the new economy, the people that companies are craving—and are willing to pay for—are people who add value to their enterprises. That means people with talent and skills and judgment.

Talent and skills and judgment are part of what economists call 'human capital'. Human capital is a broad term. It includes formal skills—for example, a degree in computer science or the ability to speak a foreign language—but it is much more than this. It also includes such things as good work habits, the judgment that comes from experience, a sense of creativity, a curiosity about the world, and the ability to think for oneself. Free societies succeed because the people who have these skills are free to use them to advance themselves, their enterprises and society.

It's true that some people manage to develop these skills on their own. For the most part, these people are highly driven self-starters. They exist in every society. They are also very rare.

For every Steve Jobs who drops out of college and founds a company like Apple, for every Jim Clark who leaves high school and starts up Netscape, for every Peter Allen who drops out and becomes a successful entertainer, there are tens of thousands of others for whom leaving school early means shutting the door forever on opportunity—and permanent condemnation to an underclass.

For most of us, the best path to success is through an education that will allow us to fulfil our potential. That begins by setting high expectations, adhering to real standards, and ensuring that when you do leave school, you leave with the tools that will help you get ahead in life.

These tools begin with the basics of any education: the ability to read and write, to add, subtract, multiply and divide, and to use these basics to acquire other, more advanced skills.

For those who doubt me, the relationship between education and opportunity is most obvious in the pay cheque. As a general rule, the more education you have, the more you are going to earn over your working career.

That differential can be very large. Two Australian economists found that for each additional year of education a person has, he can expect about 10 per cent a year in increased income. That's true even after taking into account the lost earnings from starting work later. And though that figure is for Australia, it roughly tracks with similar findings in the United States.

Even just one year of additional education can make a big difference. Here's what these economists found when they applied that 10 per cent figure to two Australian workers: the first is someone who left school at age fifteen, with nine years of education, and worked until he was sixty-four years old; the second left school at age sixteen, with ten years of education, and also retired at age sixty-four.

Over their working life, the first fellow could expect to

earn $1,166,003. The second person would earn $1,285,263. In other words, just by staying in school one more year, the second person could expect to improve his earnings by nearly $120,000.

The rewards for higher education are even more dramatic. In the United States, the educational testing service estimates that the economic advantage of a college degree is large—and growing. Today, a young person with a college degree can expect to earn nearly twice what a counterpart with a high school diploma will. Back in 1979, that difference was only 51 per cent.

Another way of putting it is this: it's not that the poor are getting poorer, it's that the economic rewards to the skilled are making them much richer. This is clearly understood by the leaders of developing countries. But it seems beyond the comprehension of much of the developed world.

This leads me to my second point: what we ought to do about it.

As the world economy grows more competitive, it will become even more difficult for people without skills to keep up. Billions of people are now entering the global workforce. A recent study by Goldman Sachs suggested that

70 million people are joining the new global middle class each year. These people are talented, they are confident, and they are increasingly well-educated.

That means the competition is getting keener. And unless we stop making excuses for our failures, a good many of our own young people will be left behind and bereft of opportunity.

Most of you are well aware of the public debate about education. And you will be well aware that there is a whole industry of pedagogues devoted to explaining why some schools and some students are failing. Some say class sizes are too large. Others complain that not enough public funding is devoted to this or that program. Still others will tell you that the students who come from certain backgrounds just can't learn.

The mediocre schools do not pay for these fundamental failings. Their students pay the price, because they are the victims when our schools fail. And the more people we graduate without basic skills, the more likely Australian society will pay the price in social dysfunction—in welfare, in healthcare, in crime. We must help ourselves by holding schools accountable and ensuring they put students on the right track.

As a rule, we spend too much time on avoiding failure. The real answer is to start pursuing success.

Developing countries seem to understand this. When I travel to places such as India and China, I do not hear people making lame excuses for mediocre schools. Instead of suggesting that their students cannot learn, they set high standards and expect they will be met. And they have crash programs for more and better schools.

The obstacles they have to overcome are as difficult and challenging as any we face here. Recently, for example, American public television ran a special called *Chinese Prep*, which followed five students through their final year at an elite high school. These students are competing for slots at the top universities in a system based almost entirely on merit.

The pressure is intense, and most Australians watching would probably think that the time and effort these boys and girls put into their studies is inhumane.

The high school in this film is elite, and it is far from representative of the schools that most Chinese attend, but the interesting thing about this show is the emphasis on competition, on merit, on doing well in standardised tests.

Some of the children who do end up doing well come from very poor backgrounds. The television cameras showed that one of them lived in what was essentially a hut in the countryside.

But no one makes allowances for them. They compete with the children of high officials. And they succeed. In a sense, the entire school system is taking a lesson from Confucius, who observed sagely, as a sage does: 'If I am walking with two other men, each of them will serve as my teacher. I will pick out the good points of the one and imitate them, and the bad points of the other and correct them in myself.'

I am not saying that Chinese education is perfect. It certainly is not. But it is clear that in a system where you are expected to perform, there is less slacking off. Maybe that's because poor people in China know that doing well in tests and getting a good education is the ticket to personal progress. Or maybe they know that the consequences for failure are much more severe than they are in, say, the more comfortable societies of America and Australia.

My point is this: the children of poor people always have fewer options than the elite. That's true whether you live in Sydney or Shanghai or San Francisco. For these people, a solid education is the one hope for rising in society and levelling the playing field. If we have any real sense of fairness, we owe these children school systems that hold them to high standards. After all, however tough their schools may be, the world is going to be even tougher and less forgiving.

That is one reason why I have two key criteria for education programs that News Corporation supports: schools must be focused on achievement, and they cannot make excuses for why some students are supposedly poor scholars.

It's amazing the results that you get when you actually expect your students to learn regardless of race, background or income. In Manhattan, for example, my wife and I have been involved with a local public school called Shuang Wen.

Shuang Wen is unique. It is the only public school in America offering a mandated bilingual program in Chinese and English for all students. Two-thirds of its students live below the poverty line. Despite this, Shuang Wen is one of New York's top-ranked schools in terms of performance. It also has the highest daily attendance rate—98 per cent.

What's the secret? In the morning, its students study in English. Then they stay until 5:30 pm to study Chinese. They come in on weekends too.

Not many American children have a school day or school week that goes as long as Shuang Wen. But instead of repelling students, the school is attracting them. African-American parents are clamouring to get their children into this school. They know that the hard work and sacrifice Shuang Wen demands of its students is their children's ticket out of poverty and hopelessness.

Another school we support in New York is the Eagle Academy for Young Men. This is what's called in America a 'charter school'. Although they are public schools, charters have more freedom than traditional American public schools. They are also directly accountable to the people who run them. The Eagle Academy for Young Men is boys-only. It was started up by a group of concerned African-American men who are simply unwilling to allow the next generation of African-American boys to be written off by the country's public schools.

Let me put this in context. The Eagle Academy has a student body of almost all Latino or African-American boys. It also operates in a part of New York City where three out of four young black men drop out before they receive a high school diploma. So failure is all around them.

But inside the Eagle Academy doors, they don't talk about failure. The students have long days, often until 6 pm. They come in on Saturdays. And they are paired with mentors. It's tough. But the results are impressive.

The fact is, the boys at Eagle Academy are getting the education they would never get from soft-hearted, supposedly well-meaning people who would just make excuses for them. And, like Shuang Wen, the Eagle Academy has a waiting list of parents who are ambitious for their children.

In Australia, our problem is a little different. In America, the children whose futures are being sacrificed tend to be those who are stuck in rotten schools in the inner cities. In Australia, by contrast, the children who suffer the most tend to be those in our rural areas and outer suburbs. But whether urban or rural, no government of any decent society should be effectively writing off whole segments of the population by refusing to confront a failing education bureaucracy.

All this leads me to my last point: corporations have an important role here. As a chief executive, I notice that many companies devote a large part of their giving to higher education. At the very critical levels of primary and secondary education there is much less corporate participation. We tend to leave that to government.

The government has an important role, of course. It will always be a key provider of money at these levels. At the

Federal level, Australia needs to set high standards for our schools—and then hold the states accountable for meeting them.

But Australian business has a role too. Companies need to take a more active part in working with government to ensure that the schools are giving people an education. As business leaders, we know how unprepared too many young people are for the working world.

My friend Bill Gates has made it one of his missions to help reform-minded school officials raise the standards at public schools. He is also supporting new models like charter schools that will provide alternatives to the one-size-fits-all model of the nineteenth century. And other corporate leaders are backing specific kinds of education, such as science and maths and computers.

At News Corporation, in addition to the individual schools I mentioned earlier, we support a leadership academy designed to train new principals, a fund for public schools, which allows the private sector to support innovative ways to expand options for schoolchildren, and New Visions for Public Schools, which has a goal to graduate in four years at least 80 per cent of our students prepared for college and work. Yet I believe we have barely scratched the surface.

In nations like Australia, we have always understood that we cannot promise that all outcomes will be equal. But at the heart of the social compact has always been the idea that everyone should have a fair go. For most citizens, we are doing this. Perhaps not as well as we can, but we are trying. But too many of our fellow Australians are being condemned to less-than-satisfying lives by a less-than-satisfactory school system.

Sometimes I think that because we are doing well enough for most people, it's easier to close our eyes to the tens of thousands of children we are betraying. We have too many people who secretly believe that the gap between those who are getting an education and those who are not is something that cannot be changed. So they blame the difference on demographics or race or utter inevitability.

The truth is this: a public school system that does not serve the least of society betrays its mission. The failure of these schools is more than a waste of human promise, and a drain on our future workforce. It is a moral scandal that no one should tolerate. A basic education—and the hope for a better life that it brings—ought to be the first civil right of any decent society.

Not all children will become neurosurgeons or computer wizards or entrepreneurs. But Australia's children are growing up in an increasingly competitive world, and they need their schools to be just as competitive. With caring adults setting high standards and insisting on accountability, all boys and girls are capable of a basic education. The need is urgent. For it is the only way they can take advantage of the tremendous opportunities this world offers, look to the future with hope, and build lives of dignity and independence.

We Australians have far to go before all will have a fair go.

five
The Global Middle
Class Roars

Poverty is not pretty, poverty is not ennobling. It is neither romantic nor rustic. We all have a responsibility to create the conditions for the poor to be less poor and then to be middle class and beyond. We all have a responsibility to challenge ideas and ideologies which have incarcerated hundreds of millions in poverty for far too long.

There is cause for modest celebration. One of the most under-reported stories of our day is the rise of a huge new global middle class. People have emerged from poverty or, I should say, have lifted themselves out of poverty, largely given this chance by global market reforms. A world dominated by a new middle class of course is not what so-called radicals had in mind a century ago when they spoke of revolution.

In 1848, a German journalist looked at the industrialised world and predicted its own destruction. 'There's a spectre haunting Europe,' he wrote. 'The spectre of communism.' Karl Marx had a newspaperman's flair for a catchy phrase. But his prediction could not have been more off target. For one thing, communism did not come via the industrialised world. Instead, the communist revolution was led by relatively underdeveloped societies, notably Russia and China.

Second, far from losing their chains, workers who lived under communist rulers were treated far worse than those in the capitalist world. The environment in these countries was degraded, and that most precious of human commodities—trust—was undermined. At the apogee of communism in China during the Cultural Revolution, neighbour did not trust neighbour, and father was alienated from son. Whatever the social idealism of communists, the reality was very different and made much of our planet almost unlivable.

One hundred and sixty years after Marx predicted revolution, a revolution is indeed changing our world, and for the better. But the revolution we see today is very different from the one he imagined. This revolution is a consequence of three billion people entering the global economy. Around the world, countries that have been blighted by civil war, political instability and communism are taking advantage of these new opportunities. The success of these once-cursed countries is a lesson for the rest of the world and for us.

Entrepreneurs and workers are creating wealth, and in the process they are fostering something many societies have never before known, a middle class linked to the global economy abroad and expanding opportunity at home. Elitists are almost dismissive of the very words 'middle class' because the fashionable have ostensible contempt for middle-class values and taste; this, despite our country being built on an egalitarian ideal, a sense that we are *all* middle class, and that to be otherwise is to be unacceptably arrogant.

In earlier chapters, I've discussed the increased competition this new global workforce means for nations like Australia. In their own countries, too, the transformation from sleepy agricultural backwaters into modern, industrial economies has brought enormous challenges. The industrial revolution in China (and that is what we are all witnessing) has created a growing middle class but also a growing environmental problem.

Yet despite the many pressures on them, leaders of once-poor nations can see the virtues of free markets. For example, they do not see the mayhem on Wall Street as a fatal flaw but, rightly, as a symptom of an excess that the system is purging. Far better to purge excess than to purge millions of innocent people.

The former UN Secretary-General, Kofi Annan, with whom I probably do not agree on many things, put it very well when he described the entry of these nations into the global economy this way: 'The main losers in today's very unequal world are not those who are too much opposed to globalisation, they are those who have been left out.' If Mr Annan is right, one of the greatest services we in rich countries can do for the poor is to open markets for their goods, and, in this, Australians can take some pride in our national record, at least in recent decades.

Through our leadership in the Cairns Group, a group of nations committed to liberalising trade in agriculture, Australia has helped open global markets to the products that poor countries actually produce. I reckon that we probably do more for poor people around the world by opening up agricultural markets than we do with all our foreign aid combined.

In some sense, globalisation is not new. A century ago, for example, the international economy was more linked, and it was in many ways easier to trade and travel. But today the reach of globalisation has been greater, its effects are more extensive, and we are far from its final phase.

The era of great globalisation began after the Second World War. In the Pacific the allied victory led to the emergence of a free and democratic Japan. This was followed by the rise of Asia's 'tiger' economies, and their success is now inspiring leaders from Belgrade to Bogota to do the same for their people. The 'tiger' economies—Hong Kong, Singapore, South Korea and Taiwan—and their dramatic successes should teach us that we should never write off a country as hopeless. None of these societies had any natural resources to speak of. Two were British colonies, the other two were part of divided nations that were more or less at war with their neighbours. They also endured decades of autocratic rule.

The 'tigers' had different governments and very different histories, but they all had one important thing in common: they relied on exports and they wanted to compete with the best companies and countries in the world. That meant that their businesses had to be internationally competitive. And we can see the results. Japan transformed itself from an imperial power to a democratic trading nation that became a model for others. Singapore faced a communist insurrection, was kicked out of the Malaysian federation and later abandoned by Britain, yet it built a wealthy society known throughout the world as the Switzerland of Asia.

Hong Kong absorbed more than a million refugees from China in the 1950s, and maintained one of the world's freest economies. As a result, these refugees were given the chance to use their resourcefulness, and eventually this former British colony surpassed Mother England in terms of per capita GDP. South Korea went from dictatorship to democracy, transforming a war-torn country into a world trading power. Like South Korea, Taiwan transformed itself from a poor nation living under a one-party rule into a world trading power and became the world's first Chinese democracy.

In more recent years, the success of Japan and the four 'tigers' has been emulated by a new group of Asian nations: Malaysia, Indonesia and Thailand. In the 1990s, the World Bank described the success of these nations in a study called 'The East Asian Miracle'. Here is how the World Bank described their economic take-off: between 1960 and 1985 real income per capita increased more than four times in Japan and the four 'tigers', and more than doubled in Indonesia, Malaysia and Thailand. If growth were randomly distributed, there is roughly one chance in 10,000 that the success would have been so regionally concentrated.

There were many factors that helped these countries turn themselves around, but the main ingredient was their openness to international markets and international competition, and their success helped pave the way for the most revolutionary development of the twentieth century: China's decision to enter the global economy.

In late 1978, Deng Xiaoping faced a China devastated by the Cultural Revolution and years of Mao's misrule. He made a courageous decision to embrace the market and end China's isolation from the world. Success did not come all at once. Deng's revolution suffered some terrible setbacks, notably Tiananmen Square, and it remains far from complete, but it is also real.

Back in the 1970s the left wing in the West was fond of the analogy of a spaceship Earth to describe the global economy. In this model, the space capsule had five astronauts. Each astronaut represented about a billion people who, when added together, equalled the world's population. One of these astronauts consumed most of the resources in the space capsule. This astronaut represented the developed world, which is said to be consuming more than its fair share of the world's resources.

What those who invoked the spaceship model never pointed out was that the same astronaut produced more than 85 per cent of those resources. The rest were producing almost nothing. If these astronauts would become as productive as the other, the world would grow fantastically richer and everyone would be better off.

And that's exactly what has been happening. China, for example, is one of these astronauts, and by every measure—diet, education, life expectancy—Chinese today are better off than their parents or grandparents. That's because after decades of punishing wealth and suppressing human capital, the Chinese have been liberated.

In a recent book called *The Elephant and the Dragon*, Robyn Meredith, a senior editor for *Forbes* magazine, focused on the rise of China. One example involving the Dutch multinational, Philips, struck me as a good metaphor for what is happening. Miss Meredith points out that Philips moved many of its lighting factories to China to cut costs. This move means lower prices for Western consumers and better profit margins for the company. But Philips' presence in China is also playing a big part in China's own development, as increased employment, for example, necessitates the building of more housing for the workforce. This in turn further benefits Philips since the more housing that is built, the more lights that Chinese people need. The same is happening with rapidly growing infrastructure needs. For example, when the Chinese government decided to modernise its highways, it needed streetlights. For Philips that meant $195 million in streetlights in 2005 alone.

Not everyone of course is sharing in this wealth. One of my nephews just returned from two years in China, where he taught English to kids in rural farm areas. Many people, he told me, might see meat only at Chinese New Year or some other holiday, but as the economy grows and the benefits reach these areas, these people will be able to increase spending on fish and meat and other sources of protein. This is already affecting the prices on our own supermarket shelves. And it's also creating untold opportunities for Australian farmers, as well as for farmers in some of the world's most impoverished countries.

In the coastal areas that have been open longest, China is seeing the rise of a middle class. Miss Meredith reports that by 2011, 290 million Chinese are expected to reach the lower rungs of the middle class. By 2025, about 520 million Chinese should reach the upper middle class. These people want the same things we do—good housing, a first-rate education for their children, and so on. Meeting this demand will be the story of our century.

The other large nation Miss Meredith writes about in her book is India. When India achieved independence from Britain in 1947, it embraced its own version of stultifying socialism. As a result, India largely cut itself off from the world. Its industries were heavily protected from outside competition and, as they became weak and outdated, experts excused the poor performance by talking of a 'Hindu rate of growth'.

There was no better symbol of India before economic reform than the Hindustan Ambassador. This is one of India's most popular cars, especially for cabbies, but in fact it is a copy of a 1956 British car, the Morris Oxford, and is still being produced today.

Now India too has opened up. I was there last July. What I saw was genuinely amazing. I met a group of ambitious young entrepreneurs who are bringing the internet to the most remote villages, giving them the same access to information that you or I have. We all feel a certain shame when we witness humiliating, avoidable poverty, but we should be equally uplifted when we see people striving to end that poverty for their families and their society.

India is becoming a world centre for innovation. Where Indian car makers were once content to produce copies of old British models, the Tata Group recently unveiled the world's most inexpensive car. Called the Nano, it is planned to sell for 100,000 Indian rupees, about A$2500, and it will put car ownership within reach of millions of newly middle-class Indians. It is hard to overestimate the impact this revolution is having on the lives of ordinary people or the role that the competition and markets have played. Miss Meredith quotes a former Indian finance secretary, who put it this way: 'We got more done for the poor by pursuing the competition agenda for a few years than we got done by pursuing a poverty agenda for decades.'

Other countries have noticed and launched their own revolutions. Look at Colombia. Until the presidential election of 2002, Colombia was a country plagued by drugs, violence and corruption. Two armed groups of Marxist rebels fought the government, and private paramilitaries were raised by the Right to fight them. Foreign investors fled, the economy sagged and the innocent were caught in the crossfire. In 2002, a charismatic leader named Álvaro Uribe Vélez ran for president, and won. In his time in office he has launched bold reforms that have taken on the drug lords, reduced corruption and expanded opportunities for the poor. As a result, Colombia last year had among the highest growth rates for all of Latin America.

Colombia is still not out of the woods. Rebel groups have not been fully defeated, the drug trade is still a problem, and the Democrats-controlled United States' Congress is holding up a pre-trade agreement with the United States. But the Colombian people are showing the world that a society that reforms and opens itself up can solve many problems that others think are intractable.

Closer to Australian shores, Vietnam is another interesting example. Vietnam's tragedy was to win a war that united the nation under communism just as communism was collapsing. So for almost two decades Vietnam slumbered while its Asian neighbours prospered. But in the 1990s Vietnam's leaders made the same decision China did and embraced the capitalist investors they used to decry. The results are beginning to show. In recent years Vietnam has been the fastest growing Asian economy after China. Ho Chi Minh City, after being almost frozen in time, is again the commercial hub of the country. Foreign investors are queuing up. The country was welcomed into the World Trade Organisation, and it is producing a middle class that is not only better fed and better dressed but also more demanding of its own government.

Like China, Vietnam has many rural citizens who are not nearly as wealthy as their urban counterparts. The country is also dealing with serious problems like double-digit inflation and state spending that makies it more expensive for people to provide the basics for their families. The government will have to make some tough decisions if it wants to keep its economy humming, and the toughest decision for any government is to transfer power from itself to its people.

I once met Prime Minister Nguyen Tan Dung. We were in Davos (Switzerland) for the World Economic Forum, surrounded by snowdrifts that you will never see on the streets of Hanoi. Mr Dung made clear that he understood the lessons of Chinese reform and promised that Vietnam would travel further down that road. He was conscious of his country's backwardness but proud of its recent achievements, and in a small symbol of that pride he wanted to show me that his smart suit, almost the equal of any on Savile Row, was made in Vietnam. His message was that Vietnam is more than capable of competing with the best of them. Every day, more of the country's 85 million people are getting the chance to prove it.

And there's Africa, a continent written off as being too hard, too difficult to reform, a basket case. Fortunately that continent is changing, and the change is coming from the most blighted of countries. Take landlocked Rwanda. Most of its people are engaged in subsistence farming and, as if this were not bad enough, in 1994 a civil war exploded into genocide that left a million dead, some at the hands of their own friends and families. If ever there was a nation with an unpromising future, Rwanda was it.

Yet Rwanda is starting to rebuild itself. Its president is a former guerrilla leader named Paul Kagame. Under his rule, national reconciliation had become a national priority. Rwandan troops have been dispatched to Darfur in Sudan because Rwandans believe they have a special role to play in stopping genocide. Rwandan voters recently became the first nation in the world to elect a female majority legislature.

At the same time, Rwanda has launched a program of privatisation and liberalisation. The aim is clear: to transform Rwanda from a nation of subsistence farmers into a modern, industrial society. No one should underestimate the challenges. The World Bank notes that most Rwandans live on less than one dollar a day, and only a tiny portion of the population has regular access to electricity and clean water. President Kagame looks at these challenges, he looks at Asia's success, and he has reached a conclusion. 'We in Africa,' he says, 'must either begin to build our scientific and technological training capabilities or remain an impoverished appendage to the global economy.' In other words, Africa needs to invest in its human capital and take its place in the global market. I like a man who thinks that way.

Rwanda has a long way to go to pull its people from desperate poverty, let alone produce a vibrant middle class but, as President Kagame appreciates, other countries have overcome difficult obstacles and they have succeeded. He believes there is no reason Rwanda cannot do the same.

Colombia, Vietnam, Rwanda—these are just a few countries that have been dismissed as hopeless but are turning themselves around. Others will have their own lists. My point is that the global economy is empowering millions of people around the earth, and as these nations rise, the global economy is going to respond to a very different set of incentives.

The reason is simple. What separates poor nations from rich nations is not talent and ability. The poor have plenty of talent and ability. Usually what people in poor nations do *not* have is the opportunity to develop their talents. That is why trade is such a powerful engine for prosperity and upward mobility. When the poor are given access to the global economy they build a better life for their families and a brighter future for their countries. And when they are successful they become something else—middle class.

In a recent study, Goldman Sachs estimated that this new global middle class is expanding by 70 million people each year. I think that 70 million could well be an underestimate. They also predict that the middle class will reach two billion more people by 2030; another underestimation by my more optimistic reckoning. But whatever the total, such a middle class means wealth and power on a scale unprecedented in human history.

Some will tell you it also means more problems. It would mean that white-collar workers in developed countries will increasingly face the same kind of threats of off-shoring that factory workers now face. It means that there will be more demand for basics like food, energy and other commodities. This increased demand coming from a new global middle class will boost competition, put new pressures on the environment and force us to change our business models.

I cannot predict how it will all turn out. It is far too easy to focus on the problems. But these vastly better-educated, better-fed groups of fellow human beings have minds as well as mouths, and everything I have experienced in my life persuades me that people living in freedom have the ability to rise to new challenges and change the world for the better. Above all, I know this: the world is in a much better place when we are dealing with the challenges of expanding prosperity rather than the miseries of expanding poverty. We should all have more faith in ourselves and in each other.

six
The Twenty-first Century: Comforting the afflicted and afflicting the comfortable

Up to this point I have shared with you my thoughts about some of the important trends and currents crashing up against our world: the challenging but ultimately liberating impact of technology; the need of my own industry to adapt to an internet age by turning newspapers into news brands that have what all great papers have—the trust and confidence of their readers; the urgent imperative of education reform, so that those without riches or connections can rise in society and build a better life for themselves and their families; and the importance of the tremendous competition to be generated by the entry into the global marketplace of billions of workers who have previously been isolated or cut off from the benefits of the international economy.

But these lectures are not about technology or newspapers or education or globalisation. They are about people and what happens when human talent, ingenuity and ambition is given free rein. Over the past six decades, the unleashing of these creative energies has raised the standard of living for hundreds of millions of people, and I believe that the opportunities before us today are even greater, bringing us to a new golden age for humankind.

Across the world, poor societies are becoming rich, and rich societies are slipping. Nations from Russia and China to Venezuela and Iran are showing the world that they resent the global status quo, and, as we are seeing, they are prepared to challenge it. Sometimes the choices these countries make leave the world more prosperous and stable, as in China's decision to join the international marketplace. Sometimes the choices these countries make leave the world a little more dangerous, as in Russia's invasion of Georgia.

In all these cases, we are talking about big changes, and the cold truth is this: Australia is not preparing itself adequately for the challenges ahead. The reason for this is also clear—we are too comfortable, and when we are comfortable we are often willing to settle for less, so long as we don't have to change how we do things. Some people who look at the changes going on elsewhere in the world will tell you that if Australia doesn't do this or doesn't do that, the consequences will be dire. I have a different message. In fact I am reasonably sure that the consequences will probably not be dire. But in my mind, that's the problem.

Today, instant flows of information, the advance of trade and the rise of economies that reward risk and enterprise are all combining to create a world where the opportunities ahead could be greater than anything we've seen in human history. Will Australia take its place in this golden age, or will we settle for the bronze, just getting by? In this time in our history, the gravest threat to Australia's freedom and prosperity does not come from war or terrorism, it comes from the comfort that can make us content.

Here is how I see it. In the twenty-first century, Australia's open economy, free society and strategic location give us many advantages. They also give us a clear choice— Australia can be a model for the world or we can be a land of squandered opportunity. That is the challenge we face. It is especially true for younger Australians.

As the chief executive of a media company that is

engaged all over this world, I have some definite opinions about where the world is heading. My view of the world owes something to my upbringing in Melbourne. I was raised in a newspaper family by a father who believed that the newspaper was among the most important instruments of human freedom. In 1947 my father said that the press must be more than merely free, it must be fact-finding and truth-seeking to the limit of human capacity and enterprise.

My father also instilled in me some guiding principles that remain with me today. These principles and the experiences I have lived through continue to shape the way I look at the world. I was born into an Australia that was a firm part of a British empire on which the sun had not yet set. I lived in a Pacific region where hundreds of millions suffered under terrible poverty and cruel dictators, and European colonialism, from Fiji to Malaya, was taken for granted. And I'm old enough to remember when sophisticated society held that these people were not fit for the democratic freedoms that we in Australia enjoyed; incidentally, a patronising idea not altogether dead yet in certain Western elites.

That old world may seem very far from the one you and I know today, but the truth is, most of the really profound changes have taken place relatively recently, and Australia's own history attests to the dramatic changes we are seeing, as borders diminish, as people claim their freedom, and as technology allows people to communicate more cheaply and efficiently than ever before.

For younger readers it must be hard to imagine what life was like just a few short decades back. You've grown up in a world where you can sit on a beach and ring a friend in Pakistan. With a click of a mouse you can send information to a mate on the other side of the world, and as long as you have access to the internet you can read about last night's footy match before you go to bed in Los Angeles.

My experience had been very different. I grew up in an Australia that did not have a national newspaper until my company, with meagre resources, started one. Remember, this was not the Dark Ages; it was 1964. Yet even allowing for these problems, Australia was coming into its own. The turning point probably started with the Second World War. Those of you who lived through those days know what I am talking about. When Singapore fell, I was ten years old. I remember how worried we all were for the Australians who were taken prisoner.

I also remember when General MacArthur arrived in Australia and made his famous vow to return to the

Philippines. (Partly I remember it because we moved out of our home in Melbourne so MacArthur's staff could use it.) As a child I saw the fear Australians experienced when the Japanese struck Darwin. More bombs were dropped there than at Pearl Harbor. At school we read about the exploits of the 'fuzzy-wuzzy angels', the ordinary people of New Guinea who risked their lives to help injured Australian troops down the Kokoda Track.

I also remember some of the more politically correct moments. For example, in June 1942 the Japanese sent their midget submarines to attack Sydney. They did not accomplish much—sinking one unarmed ship. But I recall some people in Melbourne seemed amused at the thought of all those wealthy Sydneysiders seeing the value of their beachfront property plummet. Our intercity rivalry was even stronger in those days.

The war dragged on until the atomic bomb was dropped on Japan. But the relief would be short-lived. In the 1950s we were at war with Korea. In the 1960s and 1970s it was with Vietnam. In the 1980s, the Cold War still seemed to be going strong until President Reagan faced the Russians down. Now we have a war against radical Islamic terrorists that has been going on for years. Whatever the merits of these conflicts, Australia has been involved in all of them, and it still troubles me that our citizens do not seem to appreciate the sacrifices of those who serve in our armed forces, at least not the way they do in America. That too is another legacy we would do well to change.

But my larger point is that war is not unique to our time. What is unique is the expansion of freedom. In no other age has freedom advanced as far or as fast or in such unexpected places. Nowhere has freedom changed a neighbourhood as dramatically as it has ours. Before the Second World War, the only other real democracy in our region was New Zealand, and many people thought that's how it would always be. Even though Australia was geographically situated in the Pacific, back then we were never really part of the region. Instead, we were linked to Britain, politically, economically and culturally.

Today all this has changed for the better. Japan went from being a militaristic empire that threatened to invade us to a successful democracy that is a partner for peace. Up and down the Pacific, mothers and fathers who once knew only dictatorship and misery now have children who are growing up in freedom and prosperity. Businessmen who started out with small companies have made their brands globally known for quality and value. It's easy to take these developments for granted, but back in the 1940s, anyone who dared predict this kind of future for the Asia Pacific region would have been dismissed as barking mad.

The Second World War was in many ways the transition point. Before that war, the British Empire dominated the world, and when the British competed it was with other imperial European powers who had their own colonies in the region. After the war, America came to dominate the world by American power and might, yes, but more importantly by American ideals and the opportunity and optimism that America is associated with.

To my mind, Singapore is one of the more striking examples of this change. Before the war, Singapore was thought to be impregnable, an island fortress. Then the Japanese army came down the Malaya peninsula on bicycles. The loss of Singapore was strategically devastating to the allied war effort. But it was even more devastating psychologically for the whole idea of European colonialism.

British colonialism was in many ways successful. The British ruled with a light touch and they helped bring prosperity and the rule of law to those under its dominion. Still, at bottom, British colonialism was doomed, and it was doomed because it rested on an unsustainable proposition. This was the supposed superiority of the white man. In the long run, that was an untenable notion on its own, but when Singapore fell to Japan, the British lost more than an outpost. They lost their reigning myth, and the other European powers in Asia fared no better. This wasn't obvious at first. Immediately after the war, the Europeans came back to Asia and resumed control in their former colonies. But independence movements were growing. Some were communist, some were nationalist, and all were eager to take their place in the world. They believed that history had turned.

I was given an early taste of this in 1949 when my parents and I visited Singapore. We were on our way to Britain where I was to begin university. During the war, all Australians had known shortages and deprivation, but what I saw as a young man in Singapore then was my first introduction to real, gripping poverty. You would not guess this from looking at Singapore today. But even when I see the gleaming skyscrapers and shiny cars and well-built housing, my mind turns back to the desperation and horror of Singapore after the war. There was filth everywhere, mothers carrying their babies begged for food, thousands of people lived on the streets, not knowing where their next meal would come from. Then we went up to Malaya to visit the British Commissioner-General for Southeast Asia, only to find him living in a virtual palace.

At the time I was too young to appreciate the tremendous changes on the horizon. Singapore, for example, has been successful in feeding its poor, housing its homeless and brilliantly educating the new generations. The irony is that its modern leaders seem to have some of the same worries for their city–state that I do for Australia.

In the years after the war, America played a great role in ensuring that the great ferment in the Pacific would be channelled in a mostly peaceful direction. Unlike the British, they had no territorial ambitions. Unlike the British, the end of the war had not exhausted but renewed them; and unlike the British, the Americans were willing to put their democratic ideals into practice. That led to a wonderful paradox—the man who presided over the defeat of imperial Japan, General MacArthur, would help midwife the rise of a democratic Japan.

And it worked. Within a few years, a newly democratic Japan was back on its feet and had become a global trading power. Japan's success was soon followed by Hong Kong,

Singapore, Taiwan and South Korea. Later Malaysia, Indonesia and others began to expand too. Even communist China, which suffered through starvation and chaos, began to open up. Then in the late 1970s their leader, Deng Xiaoping, a very practical man, was heard to say, 'To get rich is glorious'.

It's true that at different times some of these countries were led by home-grown dictators who treated their own people as badly as, or worse than, any colonial oppressors. But they opened up their economies for a practical reason. They understood that to survive their nations had to be competitive on global markets. This was the first real hint of globalisation.

And as people in these countries moved from poverty into the middle class, they began demanding other freedoms as well. In places like Korea, Taiwan and the Philippines they succeeded. In other parts of Asia they are still working for it.

I was a very young man when the changes that transformed our world began, and I learned some important lessons from these changes. The first is that the greatest asset a nation has is not its natural resources. The greatest asset is its people. If a nation wants to advance, the most important thing is to unlock its human potential. The only way to do that is by giving your people the freedom they need to develop their talents and abilities.

If you look around the world, you see a stark truth: free countries prosper and unfree countries do not. It's no coincidence that while the Soviet Union had some of the world's best scientists, in a society where information did not flow freely they could never realise their potential. It is also not a coincidence that when people suffering under dictatorship began to see how others lived and then compared their lot with those people in free lands, they began to demand their own freedom, and in so doing they expanded the boundaries of the possible for their compatriots and neighbours.

The Oxford of my youth was one of the most privileged places in the world, yet it was a place that had many limits. When I wrote to my parents, it would take a full week for the letter to arrive in Australia. Most people there, students as well as teachers, were white, Anglo-Saxon, Protestant males. For all our education, the prevailing outlook was narrow and provincial. Class distinctions still elevated the well-born at the expense of the talented. Above all, it was a culture that thought profit grubby and looked down on the world of business.

Across our world, millions of people are now entering university each year and enjoying an environment once limited to the very rich and well connected. Class distinctions are yielding to merit. Modern businesses are lining up with good jobs and good salaries for the talented. And far from looking down on business, many of today's students dream of starting their own. That is what freedom and information do—they democratise privilege, taking what was once something enjoyed only by the elite and making it available to more and more people.

That is the reason why even the poorest student at a school in a poor country probably has access to email and can communicate to those far away more cheaply and more efficiently than I could ever do at Oxford. That is the reason why the son of a poor farmer in Vietnam decides he needs to learn English and does; and that is the reason the daughter of a shop owner in New Delhi sets about going to graduate school abroad and achieves her goal. Some people call this ambition, as if there's something dirty about ambition. I think it's a healthy thing.

In all societies, elites have a habit of trying to kick the ladder away from those trying to climb it. Opportunity is almost universal, knowledge is everywhere and a lot of it is free, and people who were once poor are taking advantage of these changes. One benefit of growing up poor and struggling to make good is that you are probably better prepared for the competition in a global economy, and you have a sense of optimism that you don't lose when you suffer a setback or two.

For me, Australia will always be more than the land of my birth. It is the country that defined who I am, that gave me my first successes, and that still excites feelings of pride and gratitude in my heart. Today this land offers its people many more opportunities than it did when I was growing up. With so much talent, with so many advantages, and with so much potential, I can think of no greater sadness for this century than an Australia that is willing to settle for just getting by.

There was something about this country and its people and its potential that Philip Gibbs, the British war correspondent, noticed when he came across Australian troops in France, where I had three uncles in the trenches. I would have loved to think that we have remained faithful to the qualities and quirks Gibbs described. This is how he put it: 'They had no conceit of themselves in a little, vain way, but they reckoned themselves the only fighting-men, simply, and without boasting. I liked the look of them, dusty up to the eyes in summer, muddy up to their eyes in winter—these gipsy fellows, scornful of discipline for discipline's sake, but desperate fighters, looking at life with frank, curious eyes, and a kind of humorous contempt for death and disease, and "the whole damned show", as they called it.'

'The whole damned show' … We are all writing our own scripts for that show, and we should all, every woman and every man, look at life with frank, curious eyes and a kind of humorous contempt, and we should all take advantage of the opportunities that so many of those young Australians were denied so far from home.